Air Fryer Oven

Amazingly Tasty Recipes from Breakfast to Dinner to Fry, Bake, Grill, and Roast with Your Air Fryer Oven

Written By

Simona Simmons

Table of Contents

INTRODUCTION

Thank you for purchasing this book!

Saves space in your kitchen: Since you don't have to buy other appliances, you save on space in your kitchen. This is helpful especially if your kitchen is tiny. Personally, the Air Fryer is one of the two kitchen equipment that I bought when I was living in a very small flat. It saved me a lot of space in the kitchen.

Enjoy your reading!

BREAKFAST

Tarragon and Parmesan Scramble

Preparation Time: 25 minutes

Servings: 4

Ingredients:

8 eggs; whisked

¼ cup coconut cream

2 tbsp. parmesan; grated

2 tbsp. tarragon; chopped.

Salt and black pepper to taste.

Directions:

Take a bowl and mix the eggs with all the ingredients and whisk.

Pour this into a pan that fits your air fryer, introduce it in the preheated fryer and cook at 350°F for 20 minutes, stirring often

Divide the scramble between plates and serve for breakfast.

Nutrition: Calories: 221; Fat: 12g; Fiber: 4g; Carbs: 5g; Protein: 9g

Creamy Spinach Spread

Preparation Time: 15 minutes

Servings: 4

Ingredients:

3 cups spinach leaves

2 tbsp. bacon, cooked and crumbled

2 tbsp. coconut cream

2 tbsp. cilantro

Salt and black pepper to taste.

Directions:

In a pan that fits the air fryer, combine all the ingredients except the bacon, put the pan in the machine and cook at 360°F for 10 minutes

Transfer to a blender, pulse well, divide into bowls and serve with bacon sprinkled on top.

Nutrition: Calories: 200; Fat: 4g; Fiber: 2g; Carbs: 4g; Protein: 4g

Salmon Eggs

Preparation Time: 25 minutes

Servings: 4

Ingredients:

1 cup smoked salmon, skinless; boneless and flaked

¼ cup baby spinach

4 eggs; whisked

A drizzle of olive oil

1 spring onion; chopped.

A pinch of salt and black pepper

4 tbsp. parmesan; grated

Directions:

Take a bowl and mix the eggs with the rest of the ingredients except the oil and whisk well.

Grease the Air Fryer with the oil, preheat it at 360°F, pour the eggs and salmon mix and cook for 20 minutes.

Divide between plates and serve for breakfast

Nutrition: Calories: 230; Fat: 12g; Fiber: 3g; Carbs: 5g; Protein: 12g

Yogurt Omelet

Preparation Time: 25 minutes

Servings: 4

Ingredients:

1 ½ cups Greek yogurt

4 eggs; whisked

1 tbsp. cilantro; chopped.

1 tbsp. chives; chopped.

Cooking spray

Salt and black pepper to taste.

Directions:

Take a bowl and mix all the ingredients except the cooking spray and whisk well.

Now, take a pan that fits in your air fryer and grease it with the cooking spray, pour the eggs mix, spread well, put the pan into the machine and cook the omelet at 360°F for 20 minutes. Divide between plates and serve for breakfast

Nutrition: Calories: 221; Fat: 14g; Fiber: 4g; Carbs: 6g; Protein: 11g

Green Beans and Radish Salad

Preparation Time: 20 minutes

Servings: 4

Ingredients:

½ lb. green beans; trimmed

4 eggs; whisked

1 ¾ cups radishes; chopped.

1 tbsp. cilantro; chopped.

A pinch of salt and black pepper

Cooking spray

Directions:

Now, take a pan that fits in your air fryer and grease it with the cooking spray, add all the ingredients, toss and cook at 360°F for 15 minutes

Divide between plates and serve for breakfast.

Nutrition: Calories: 212; Fat: 12g; Fiber: 3g; Carbs: 4g; Protein: 9g

LUNCH

Grilled Chicken with Garlic Sauce

Preparation Time: 15-minutes

Servings: 4

Ingredients:

1lb. chicken breast, cut into large cubes

2 bell peppers, chopped

1 zucchini

1 onion, chopped

For Garlic Sauce:

1 head garlic, peeled

¼ cup lemon juice

1 cup olive oil

1 teaspoon salt

Additional ingredients for the marinade:

1 teaspoon salt

½ cup olive oil

Directions:

Soak 4 wooden skewers in water. For your garlic sauce, place garlic cloves and salt into blender. Then, add in about 1/8 of a cup of lemon juice and ½ a cup of olive oil. Blend for about 10-seconds. Keep half of the garlic sauce to serve with. Take the other half of garlic sauce and add an additional ½ cup of olive oil and a teaspoon of salt and mix well—this will make your marinade. Chop up the chicken, onion, bell peppers, and zucchini into 1-inch cubes or squares. Mix them in a bowl with the marinade. Place the cubes onto the skewers and cook them directly on the air fryer rack at 400°Fahrenheit for 15-minutes. Serve warm.

Nutrition: Calories: 321, Total Fat: 12.5g, Carbs: 9.2g, Protein: 32.1g

Bacon-Wrapped Stuffed Zucchini Boats

Preparation Time: 15 minutes

Servings: 4

Ingredients:

½ a teaspoon of fresh ground black pepper

1 teaspoon sea salt

5-ounces cream cheese

8-mushrooms, finely chopped

1 tablespoon Italian parsley, chopped

1 tablespoon finely chopped dill

3 garlic cloves, peeled, pressed

1 sweet red pepper, finely chopped

2 large zucchinis

12 bacon strips

1 medium onion, chopped

Directions:

Preheat your air fryer to 350°Fahrenheit. Trim the ends off zucchini. Cut zucchini in half lengthwise. Scoop out pulp, leaving ¼-inch thick shells. Stir pulp in mixing bowl. Add onion, garlic, herbs, pepper, cream cheese, salt, and pepper. Mix well to combine. Fill individual shells with the same amount of stuffing. Wrap three bacon strips around each zucchini boat such that the ends end up underneath. Place them directly on the air fryer rack and bake turning the temperature up to 375°Fahrenheit for 15-minutes. Remove and serve immediately.

Nutrition: Calories: 282, Total Fat: 9.1g, Carbs: 6.3g, Protein: 24.2g

Parmesan Chicken Wings

Preparation Time: 22 minutes

Servings: 4

Ingredients:

2 lbs. chicken wings

2 tablespoons olive oil

1 teaspoon sea salt

1 teaspoon black pepper

3 tablespoons butter

3 tablespoons olive oil

3 garlic cloves, minced

4 tablespoons parmesan cheese

1/8 teaspoon smoked paprika

¼ teaspoon red pepper flakes

Salt and pepper to taste

Directions:

Add chicken to a bowl and pat the chicken dry. Drizzle with 2 tablespoons of olive oil, 1 teaspoon of sea salt, and 1 teaspoon black pepper. Gently toss to coat chicken. Place chicken wings into air fryer directly on the rack. Bake at 400°Fahrenheit for 20-minutes, flipping wings half-way through cook time. In a pan over medium heat add butter and 3 tablespoons olive oil and melt the butter down, for about 3-minutes. Add 2 tablespoons of parmesan cheese, smoked paprika, red pepper flakes, salt and pepper to taste. Cook sauce for about 2-minutes. Remove the wings from air fryer and place in large bowl. Pour the garlic parmesan sauce over the wings toss to coat. Serve wings topped with additional a2 tablespoons of parmesan cheese.

Nutrition: Calories: 324, Total Fat: 12.3g, Carbs: 9.3g, Protein: 39.3g

Beef Burgers

Preparation Time: 10 minutes

Servings: 4

Ingredients:

1 lb. ground beef

1 teaspoon parsley, dried

½ teaspoon oregano, dried

½ teaspoon ground black pepper

½ teaspoon salt

½ teaspoon onion powder

½ teaspoon garlic powder

1 tablespoon Worcestershire sauce

Olive oil cooking spray

Directions:

In a mixing bowl, mix the seasonings. Add the seasoning to beef in a bowl. Mix well to combine. Divide the beef into four patties, put an indent in the middle of patties with your thumb to prevent patties from bunching up in the middle. Place burgers into air fryer and spray the tops of them with olive oil. Cook for 10-minutes at 400°Fahrenheit, no need to flip patties. Serve on a bun with a side dish of your choice.

Nutrition: Calories: 312, Total Fat: 11.3g, Carbs: 7.2g, Protein: 39.2g

DINNER

Zucchini and Cauliflower Stew

Preparation Time: 25 minutes

Servings: 4

Ingredients:

1 cauliflower head, florets separated

1 ½ cups zucchinis; sliced

1 handful parsley leaves; chopped.

½ cup tomato puree

2 green onions; chopped.

1 tbsp. balsamic vinegar

1 tbsp. olive oil

Salt and black pepper to taste.

Directions:

In a pan that fits your air fryer, mix the zucchinis with the rest of the ingredients except the parsley, toss, introduce the pan in the air fryer and cook at 380°F for 20 minutes

Divide into bowls and serve for lunch with parsley sprinkled on top.

Nutrition: Calories: 193; Fat: 5g; Fiber: 2g; Carbs: 4g; Protein: 7g

Lemony Chicken Thighs

Preparation Time: 45 minutes

Servings: 6

Ingredients:

3 lb. chicken thighs, bone-in

1 tbsp. smoked paprika

½ cup butter; melted

1 tsp. lemon juice

Directions:

Take a bowl and mix the chicken thighs with the paprika, toss, put all the pieces in your air fryer's basket and cook them at 360°F for 25 minutes shaking the fryer from time to time and basting the meat with the butter.

Divide between plates and serve

Nutrition: Calories: 261; Fat: 16g; Fiber: 3g; Carbs: 5g; Protein: 12g

Okra and Zucchini Stew

Preparation Time: 25 minutes

Servings: 4

Ingredients:

4 zucchinis, roughly cubed

7 oz. tomato sauce

2 green bell peppers; cut into strips

2 garlic cloves; minced

1 cup okra

2 tbsp. olive oil

2 tbsp. cilantro; chopped.

1 tsp. oregano; dried

Salt and black pepper to taste.

Directions:

In a pan that fits your air fryer, combine all the ingredients for the stew, toss, introduce the pan in the air fryer, cook the stew at 350°F for 20 minutes

Divide into bowls and serve.

Nutrition: Calories: 230; Fat: 5g; Fiber: 2g; Carbs: 4g; Protein: 8g

Fennel and Tomato Stew

Preparation Time: 25 minutes

Servings: 4

Ingredients:

2 fennel bulbs; shredded

½ cup chicken stock

1 red bell pepper; chopped.

2 garlic cloves; minced

2 cups tomatoes; cubed

2 tbsp. tomato puree

1 tsp. rosemary; dried

1 tsp. sweet paprika

Salt and black pepper to taste.

Directions:

In a pan that fits your air fryer, mix all the ingredients, toss, introduce in the fryer and cook at 380°F for 15 minutes

Divide the stew into bowls.

Nutrition: Calories: 184; Fat: 7g; Fiber: 2g; Carbs: 3g; Protein: 8g

Tomato Stew

Preparation Time: 20 minutes

Servings: 4

Ingredients:

25 oz. canned tomatoes; cubed

4 spring onions; chopped.

2 red bell peppers; cubed

1 tbsp. cilantro; chopped.

1 tsp. sweet paprika

Salt and black pepper to taste.

Directions:

In a pan that fits your air fryer, mix all the ingredients, toss, introduce the pan in the fryer and cook at 360°F for 15 minutes

Divide into bowls and serve.

Nutrition: Calories: 185; Fat: 3g; Fiber: 2g; Carbs: 4g; Protein: 9g

PARTIES & SPECIAL EVENTS

Skirt Steak with Veggies

Servings: 4

Preparation Time: 15 minutes

Cooking Time: 6 minutes

Ingredients

¼ cup olive oil, divided

2 tablespoons soy sauce

2 tablespoons honey

1 (12-ouncesskirt steak, cut into thin strips

½ pound fresh mushrooms, quartered

6 ounces snow peas

1 onion, cut into half rings

Salt and ground black pepper, as required

Directions:

In a bowl, mix together 2 tablespoons of oil, soy sauce, and honey.
Add the steak strips and generously coat with the oil mixture.
In another bowl, add the vegetables, remaining oil, salt, and black pepper.
Toss to coat well.
Set the temperature of air fryer to 390 degrees F. Grease an air fryer
basket.

Arrange steak strips and vegetables into the prepared air fryer basket.

Air fry for about 5-6 minutes or until desired doneness.

Remove from air fryer and place the steak onto a cutting board for about 10 minutes before slicing.

Cut each steak into desired size slices and transfer onto serving plates.

Serve immediately alongside the veggies.

Nutrition:

Calories: 360

Carbohydrate: 16.7g

Protein: 26.7g

Fat: 21.5g

Sugar: 12.6g

Sodium: 522mg

Steak with Bell Peppers

Servings: 4

Preparation Time: 20 minutes

Cooking Time: 22 minutes

Ingredients

1 teaspoon dried oregano, crushed

1 teaspoon onion powder

1 teaspoon garlic powder

1 teaspoon red chili powder

1 teaspoon paprika

Salt, to taste

1¼ pounds beef steak, cut into thin strips

2 green bell peppers, seeded and cubed

1 red bell pepper, seeded and cubed

1 red onion, sliced

2 tablespoons olive oil

Directions:

In a large bowl, mix together the oregano and spices.

Add the beef strips, bell peppers, onion, and oil. Mix until well combined.

Set the temperature of air fryer to 390 degrees F. Grease an air fryer basket.

Arrange steak strips mixture into the prepared Air Fryer basket in 2 batches.

Air Fry for about 10-11 minutes or until done completely.

Remove from air fryer and transfer the steak mixture onto serving plates.

Serve immediately.

Nutrition:

Calories: 372

Carbohydrate: 11.2g

Protein: 44.6g

Fat: 16.3g

Sugar: 6.2g

Sodium: 143mg

Buttered Filet Mignon

Servings: 4

Preparation Time: 10 minutes

Cooking Time: 14 minutes

Ingredients

2 (6-ouncesfilet mignon steaks

1 tablespoon butter, softened

Salt and ground black pepper, as required

Directions:

Coat each steak evenly with butter and then, season with salt and black pepper.

Set the temperature of air fryer to 390 degrees F. Grease an air fryer basket.

Arrange steaks into the prepared air fryer basket.

Air fry for about 14 minutes, flipping once halfway through.

Remove from the air fryer and transfer onto serving plates.

Serve hot.

Nutrition:

Calories: 403

Carbohydrate: 0g

Protein: 48.7g

Fat: 22g

Sugar: 0g

Sodium: 228mg

Bacon Wrapped Filet Mignon

Servings: 2

Preparation Time: 15 minutes

Cooking Time: 15 minutes

Ingredients

2 bacon slices

2 (6-ouncesfilet mignon steaks

Salt and ground black pepper, as required

1 teaspoon avocado oil

Directions:

Wrap 1 bacon slice around each mignon steak and secure with a toothpick.

Season the steak evenly with salt and black pepper.

Then, coat each steak with avocado oil.

Set the temperature of air fryer to 375 degrees F. Grease an air fryer basket.

Arrange steaks into the prepared air fryer basket.

Air fry for about 15 minutes, flipping once halfway through.

Remove from air fryer and transfer the steaks onto serving plates.

Serve hot.

Nutrition:

Calories: 512

Carbohydrate: 0.5g

Protein: 59.4g

Fat: 28.6g

Sugar: 0g

Sodium: 857mg

Beef Short Ribs

Servings: 8

Preparation Time: 15 minutes

Cooking Time: 16 minutes

Ingredients

4 pounds bone-in beef short ribs

1/3 cup scallions, chopped

1 tablespoon fresh ginger, finely grated

1 cup low-sodium soy sauce

½ cup rice vinegar

1 tablespoon Sriracha

2 tablespoons brown sugar

1 teaspoon ground black pepper

Directions:

In a resealable bag, put the ribs and all the above ingredients.

Seal the bag and shake to coat well.

Refrigerate overnight.

Set the temperature of air fryer to 380 degrees F. Grease an air fryer basket.

Take out the short ribs from resealable bag and arrange into the prepared air fryer basket in 2 batches in a single layer.

Air Fry for about 8 minutes, flipping once halfway through.

Remove from air fryer and transfer onto a serving platter.

Serve hot.

Nutrition:

Calories: 507

Carbohydrate: 6.3g

Protein: 67.3g

Fat: 20.5g

Sugar: 2.8g

Sodium: 1200mg

Herbed Beef Roast

Servings: 5

Preparation Time: 10 minutes

Cooking Time: 45 minutes

Ingredients

2 pounds beef roast

1 tablespoon olive oil

1 teaspoon dried rosemary, crushed

1 teaspoon dried thyme, crushed

Salt, as required

Directions:

In a bowl, mix together the oil, herbs, and salt.

Generously coat the roast with herb mixture.

Set the temperature of air fryer to 360 degrees F. Grease an air fryer basket.

Arrange roast into the prepared air fryer basket.

Air fry for about 45 minutes.

Remove from air fryer and transfer the roast onto a platter.

With a piece of foil, cover the roast for about 10 minutes before slicing.

Cut the roast into desired size slices and serve.

Nutrition:

Calories: 362

Carbohydrate: 0.3g

Protein: 55.1g

Fat: 14.2g

Sugar: 0g

Sodium: 151mg

VEGAN RECIPES

Roasted Asparagus

Preparation Time: 15 minutes

Servings: 4

Ingredients:

1 lb. asparagus, trimmed

1 tbsp. sweet paprika

3 tbsp. olive oil

A pinch of salt and black pepper

Directions:

Take a bowl and mix the asparagus with the rest of the ingredients and toss

Put the asparagus in your air fryer's basket and cook at 400°F for 10 minutes. Divide between plates and serve

Nutrition: Calories: 200; Fat: 5g; Fiber: 2g; Carbs: 4g; Protein: 6g

Portobello Mini Pizzas

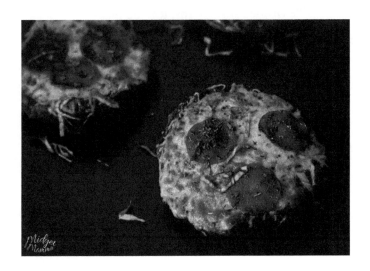

Preparation Time: 20 minutes

Servings: 2

Ingredients:

2 large portobello mushrooms

2 leaves fresh basil; chopped

⅔ cup shredded mozzarella cheese

4 grape tomatoes, sliced

1 tbsp. balsamic vinegar

2 tbsp. unsalted butter; melted.

½ tsp. garlic powder.

Directions:

Scoop out the inside of the mushrooms, leaving just the caps. Brush each cap with butter and sprinkle with garlic powder.

Fill each cap with mozzarella and sliced tomatoes. Place each mini pizza into a 6-inch round baking pan. Place pan into the air fryer basket.

Adjust the temperature to 380 Degrees F and set the timer for 10 minutes

Carefully remove the pizzas from the fryer basket and garnish with basil and a drizzle of vinegar.

Nutrition: Calories: 244; Protein: 10.4g; Fiber: 1.4g; Fat: 18.5g; Carbs: 6.8g

Asparagus and Tomatoes

Preparation Time: 15 minutes

Servings: 4

Ingredients:

1 lb. asparagus, trimmed

½ cup balsamic vinegar

2 cups cherry tomatoes; halved

¼ cup parmesan, grated

2 tbsp. olive oil

A pinch of salt and black pepper

Directions:

Take a bowl and mix the asparagus with the rest of the ingredients except the parmesan and toss.

Put the asparagus and tomatoes in your air fryer's basket and cook at 400°F for 10 minutes

Divide between plates and serve with the parmesan sprinkled on top.

Nutrition: Calories: 173; Fat: 4g; Fiber: 2g; Carbs: 4g; Protein: 8g

Nutmeg Endives

Preparation Time: 15 minutes

Servings: 4

Ingredients:

4 endives, trimmed and halved

1 tbsp. lemon juice

1 tbsp. chives; chopped.

1 tbsp. coconut oil; melted

½ tsp. nutmeg, ground

Salt and black pepper to taste.

Directions:

Take a bowl and mix the endives with the rest of the ingredients except the chives and toss well.

Put the endives in your air fryer's basket and cook at 360°F for 10 minutes

Divide the endives between plates, sprinkle the chives on top and serve.

Nutrition: Calories: 162; Fat: 4g; Fiber: 3g; Carbs: 5g; Protein: 7g

Almond Butter Cookie Balls

Preparation Time: 15 minutes

Servings: 10 balls

Ingredients:

1 cup almond butter

1 large egg.

¼ cup powdered erythritol

¼ cup shredded unsweetened coconut

¼ cup low-carb, sugar-free chocolate chips.

¼ cup low-carb protein powder

½ tsp. ground cinnamon.

1 tsp. vanilla extract.

Directions:

Take a large bowl, mix almond butter and egg. Add in vanilla, protein powder and erythritol.

Fold in coconut, chocolate chips and cinnamon. Roll into 1-inch balls. Place balls into 6-inch round baking pan and put into the air fryer basket

Adjust the temperature to 320 Degrees F and set the timer for 10 minutes

Allow to cool completely. Store in an airtight container in the refrigerator up to 4 days.

Nutrition: Calories: 224; Protein: 11.2g; Fiber: 3.6g; Fat: 16.0g; Carbs: 14.9g

BEGINNERS

Tender Beef Chuck with Brussels Sprouts

Preparation Time: 25 minutes + marinating time

Servings: 4

Nutrition: 302 Calories; 14.2g Fat; 6.5g Carbs; 36.6g Protein; 1.6g Sugars

Ingredients

1-pound beef chuck shoulder steak

2 tablespoons vegetable oil

1 tablespoon red wine vinegar

1 teaspoon fine sea salt

1/2 teaspoon ground black pepper

1 teaspoon smoked paprika

1 teaspoon onion powder

1/2 teaspoon garlic powder

1/2-pound Brussels sprouts, cleaned and halved

1/2 teaspoon fennel seeds

1 teaspoon dried basil

1 teaspoon dried sage

Directions

Firstly, marinate the beef with vegetable oil, wine vinegar, salt, black pepper, paprika, onion powder, and garlic powder. Rub the marinade into the meat and let it stay at least for 3 hours.

Air fry at 390 degrees F for 10 minutes. Pause the machine and add the prepared Brussels sprouts; sprinkle them with fennel seeds, basil, and sage.

Turn the machine to 380 degrees F; press the power button and cook for 5 more minutes. Pause the machine, stir and cook for further 10 minutes.

Next, remove the meat from the cooking basket and cook the vegetables a few minutes more if needed and according to your taste. Serve with your favorite mayo sauce.

All-In-One Spicy Spaghetti with Beef

Preparation Time: 30 minutes

Servings: 4

Nutrition: 359 Calories; 5.5g Fat; 59.9g Carbs; 16.9g Protein; 2.7g Sugars

Ingredients

3/4-pound ground chuck

1 onion, peeled and finely chopped

1 teaspoon garlic paste

1 bell pepper, chopped

1 small-sized habanero pepper, deveined and finely minced

1/2 teaspoon dried rosemary

1/2 teaspoon dried marjoram

1 ¼ cups crushed tomatoes, fresh or canned

1/2 teaspoon sea salt flakes

1/4 teaspoon ground black pepper, or more to taste

1 package cooked spaghetti, to serve

Directions

In the Air Fryer baking dish, place the ground meat, onion, garlic paste, bell pepper, habanero pepper, rosemary, and the marjoram.

Air-fry, uncovered, for 10 to 11 minutes. Next step stirs in the tomatoes along with salt and pepper; cook 17 to 20 minutes. Serve over cooked spaghetti. Bon appétit!

Beer-Braised Short Loin

Preparation Time: 15 minutes

Servings: 4

Nutrition: 379 Calories; 16.4g Fat; 3.7g Carbs; 46.0g Protein; 0.0g Sugars

Ingredients

1 ½ pounds short loin

2 tablespoons olive oil

1 bottle beer

2-3 cloves garlic, finely minced

2 Turkish bay leaves

Directions

Pat the beef dry; then, tenderize the beef with a meat mallet to soften the fibers. Place it in a large-sized mixing dish.

Add the remaining ingredients; toss to coat well and let it marinate for at least 1 hour.

Cook about 7 minutes at 395 degrees F; after that, pause the Air Fryer. Flip the meat over and cook for another 8 minutes, or until it's done.

Beef and Kale Omelet

Preparation Time: 20 minutes

Servings: 4

Nutrition: 236 Calories; 13.7g Fat; 4.0g Carbs; 23.8g Protein; 1.0g Sugars

Ingredients

Non-stick cooking spray

1/2-pound leftover beef, coarsely chopped

2 garlic cloves, pressed

1 cup kale, torn into pieces and wilted

1 tomato, chopped

1/4 teaspoon brown sugar

4 eggs, beaten

4 tablespoons heavy cream

1/2 teaspoon turmeric powder

Salt and ground black pepper, to your liking

1/8 teaspoon ground allspice

Directions

Spritz the inside of four ramekins with a cooking spray.

Divide all the above ingredients among the prepared ramekins. Stir until everything is well combined.

Air-fry at 360 degrees F for 16 minutes; check with a wooden stick and return the eggs to the Air Fryer for a few more minutes as needed. Serve immediately.

Delicious Turkey Sammies

Preparation Time: 50 minutes

Servings: 4

Nutrition: 452 Calories; 24.8g Fat; 22.9g Carbs; 38.5g Protein; 9.1g Sugars

Ingredients

1/2-pound turkey tenderloins

1 tablespoon olive oil

Salt and ground black pepper, to your liking

4 slices bread

1/4 cup tomato paste

1/4 cup pesto sauce

1 yellow onion, thinly sliced

1 cup mozzarella cheese, shredded

Directions

Brush the turkey tenderloins with olive oil. Season with salt and black pepper.

Cook the turkey tenderloins at 350 degrees F for 30 minutes, flipping them over halfway through. Let them rest for 5 to 9 minutes before slicing.

Cut the turkey tenderloins into thin slices. Make your sandwiches with bread, tomato paste, pesto, and onion. Place the turkey slices on top. Add the cheese and place the sandwiches in the Air Fryer basket.

Then, preheat your Air Fryer to 390 degrees F. Bake for 7 minutes or until cheese is melted. Serve immediately.

Mexican-Style Brown Rice Casserole

Preparation Time: 50 minutes

Servings: 4

Nutrition: 433 Calories; 7.4g Fat; 79.6g Carbs; 12.1g Protein; 2.8g Sugars

Ingredients

1 tablespoon olive oil

1 shallot, chopped

2 cloves garlic, minced

1 habanero pepper, minced

2 cups brown rice

3 cups chicken broth

1 cup water

2 ripe tomatoes, pureed

Sea salt and ground black pepper, to taste

1/2 teaspoon dried Mexican oregano

1 teaspoon red pepper flakes

1 cup Mexican Cotija cheese, crumbled

Directions

In a nonstick skillet, heat the olive oil over a moderate flame. Once hot, cook the shallot, garlic, and habanero pepper until tender and fragrant; reserve.

Heat the brown rice, vegetable broth and water in a pot over high heat. Bring it to a boil; turn the stove down to simmer and cook for 35 minutes.

Grease a baking pan with nonstick cooking spray.

Spoon the cooked rice into the baking pan. Add the sautéed mixture. Spoon the tomato puree over the sautéed mixture. Sprinkle with salt, black pepper, oregano, and red pepper.

Cook in the preheated Air Fryer at 380 degrees F for 8 minutes. Top with the Cotija cheese and bake for 5 minutes longer or until cheese is melted. Enjoy!

FAST RECIPES

Cheesy Ravioli and Marinara Sauce

Preparation Time: 18 Minutes

Servings: 6

Ingredients:

20 oz. cheese ravioli

10 oz. marinara sauce

1/4 cup parmesan; grated

1 tbsp. olive oil

1 cup buttermilk

2 cups breadcrumbs

Directions:

Put buttermilk in a bowl and breadcrumbs in another bowl.

Dip ravioli in buttermilk, then in breadcrumbs and place them in your air fryer on a baking sheet. Drizzle olive oil over them; cook at 400 °F, for 5 minutes; divide them on plates, sprinkle parmesan on top and serve for lunch

Nutrition: Calories: 270; Fat: 12; Fiber: 6; Carbs: 30; Protein: 15

Chicken Kabobs

Preparation Time: 30 Minutes

Servings: 2

Ingredients:

2 chicken breasts; skinless, boneless and roughly cubed

3 orange bell peppers; cut into squares

1/4 cup honey

1/3 cup soy sauce

Cooking spray

6 mushrooms; halved

Salt and black pepper to the taste

Directions:

In a bowl; mix chicken with salt, pepper, honey, say sauce and some cooking spray and toss well.

Thread chicken, bell peppers and mushrooms on skewers; place them in your air fryer and cook at 338 °F, for 20 minutes. Divide among plates and serve for lunch.

Nutrition: Calories: 261; Fat: 7; Fiber: 9; Carbs: 12; Protein: 6

Stuffed Portobello Mushrooms

Preparation Time: 30 Minutes

Servings: 4

Ingredients:

4 big Portobello mushroom caps

1/3 cup breadcrumbs

1/4 tsp. rosemary; chopped.

1 tbsp. olive oil

1/4 cup ricotta cheese

5 tbsp. parmesan; grated

1 cup spinach; torn

Directions:

Rub mushrooms caps with the oil; place them in your air fryer's basket and cook them at 350 °F, for 2 minutes.

Meanwhile; in a bowl, mix half of the parmesan with ricotta, spinach, rosemary and breadcrumbs and stir well.

Stuff mushrooms with this mix; sprinkle the rest of the parmesan on top; place them in your air fryer's basket again and cook at 350 °F, for 10 minutes. Divide them on plates and serve with a side salad for lunch.

Nutrition: Calories: 152; Fat: 4; Fiber: 7; Carbs: 9; Protein: 5

RECIPES FOR TWO

Creamy Tilapia

Preparation Time: 12 minutes

Cooking time: 16 minutes

Servings: 2

Ingredients

¼ cup cream

15 oz tilapia fillet

½ teaspoon garlic, sliced

¼ teaspoon ground coriander

1 teaspoon fresh thyme

½ teaspoon butter

Directions:

Put the tilapia fillet in the bowl.

Sprinkle it with the sliced garlic, ground coriander, and fresh thyme.

Add cream and stir the fish well.

Preheat the air fryer to 360 F.

Toss the butter in the air fryer basket and melt it.

Then put the tilapia fillet in the melted butter.

Sprinkle it with the remaining cream mixture and cook for 16 minutes.

Flip the tilapia fillet into another side after 8 minutes of cooking.

Transfer the cooked tilapia to the serving plate.

Enjoy!

Nutrition: calories 205, fat 4.6, fiber 0.2, carbs 1.5, protein 39.9

Beer Cod

Preparation Time: 20 minutes

Cooking time: 10 minutes

Servings: 2

Ingredients

½ cup beer

¼ teaspoon salt

½ teaspoon ground black pepper

14 oz cod fillet

4 tablespoon breadcrumbs

1 tablespoon Italian seasoning

½ teaspoon olive oil

1 egg

Directions:

Sprinkle the cod fillet with the salt and ground black pepper.

Then put the cod fillet in the beer and leave it for 10 minutes.

Meanwhile, combine the breadcrumbs and Italian seasoning in the

bowl. Stir the mixture.

Crack the egg into the bowl and whisk it.

Remove the fish fillet from the beer and cut it into 2 parts.

Then dip the fish pieces into the egg mixture.

After this, sprinkle the fish pieces with the breadcrumb mixture.

Preheat the air fryer to 400 F.

Put the fish pieces in the air fryer tray and sprinkle them with the olive oil.

Cook the fish fillet for 4 minutes.

After this, flip the fish fillets to another side and cook them for 6 minutes.

Serve the cooked fish immediately.

Enjoy!

Nutrition: calories 264, fat 7.5, fiber 0.8, carbs 13.1, protein 31.7

Garlic Catfish

Preparation Time: 18 minutes

Cooking time: 9 minutes

Servings: 2

Ingredients

14 oz catfish

2 teaspoon minced garlic

1 teaspoon olive oil

½ teaspoon butter

½ teaspoon dried dill

½ teaspoon dried parsley

1 teaspoon onion powder

½ teaspoon garlic powder

Directions:

Rub the catfish with the minced garlic.

Then combine the olive oil with the dried dill, dried parsley, onion powder, and garlic powder.

Whisk it until homogenous.

Then brush the catfish with the oil mixture.

Leave the catfish for 10 minutes to marinate.

Preheat the air fryer to 400 F.

Melt the butter in the air fryer and put the catfish there.

Cook the catfish for 6 minutes.

After this, flip the fish to another side and cook for 3 minutes more.

When the fish is cooked – let it chill briefly.

Enjoy!

Nutrition: calories 494, fat 29.8, fiber 1.6, carbs 18.5, protein 36.4

Lemon Snapper

Preparation Time: 20 minutes

Cooking time: 12 minutes

Servings: 2

Ingredients

12 oz snapper

½ lemon

2 garlic cloves

½ yellow onion

¼ teaspoon ground thyme

¼ teaspoon turmeric

½ teaspoon dried dill

1 tablespoon fresh parsley

1 teaspoon olive oil

1 teaspoon butter

Directions:

Slice the lemon.

Dice the yellow onion and chop the garlic cloves.

Rub the snapper with the ground thyme, turmeric, dried dill, and olive oil.

Massage the fish gently.

After this, fill the snapper with the fresh dill and better.

Make the small cuts on the surface of the fish and put the sliced lemon into the cuts.

Preheat the air fryer to 365 F.

Put the snapper in the air fryer basket and cook the fish for 12 minutes.

Check if the fish is cooked and discard it from the air fryer basket.

After this, cut the fish into 2 servings.

Enjoy!

Nutrition: calories 279, fat 7.4, fiber 1.3, carbs 5.4, protein 44.8

Orange Beef Mignon

Preparation Time: 30 minutes

Cooking time: 18 minutes

Servings: 2

Ingredients

15 oz beef mignon

1 orange

½ teaspoon white pepper

½ teaspoon ground black pepper

1 teaspoon olive oil

¼ teaspoon ground thyme

¼ teaspoon dried cilantro

Directions:

Grate the zest from the orange.

After this, squeeze juice from the orange.

Cut the beef into 2 servings.

Combine the orange juice, orange zest, white pepper, ground black pepper, olive oil, ground thyme, and dried cilantro.

Mix it and dip the beef there.

Leave the beef for 20 minutes to marinate in the fridge.

Preheat the air fryer to 400 F.

Put the beef mignons in the air fryer and sprinkle with ½ part of orange juice mixture.

Cook the meat for 18 minutes.

When the beef mignon is cooked – transfer the meal to the serving plates.

Taste it.

Nutrition: calories 380, fat 17.2, fiber 2.4, carbs 11.2, protein 42

Chicken Schnitzel

Preparation Time: 10 minutes

Cooking time: 13 minutes

Servings: 2

Ingredients

2 chicken fillets

½ teaspoon salt

½ teaspoon ground black pepper

1 egg

¼ cup oatmeal flour

½ teaspoon olive oil

Directions:

Beat the chicken fillets well.

Then sprinkle the chicken fillets with the salt and ground black pepper from each side.

Crack the egg into the bowl and whisk it.

Dip the chicken fillets in the whisked egg.

Then coat the chicken in the oatmeal flour.

Preheat the air fryer to 355 F.

Put the chicken fillets on the air fryer tray and spray them with the olive oil.

Cook the schnitzels for 13 minutes.

Flip the chicken to another side after 6 minutes of cooking.

Serve the cooked schnitzels hot.

Enjoy!

Nutrition: calories 303, fat 14.9, fiber 2, carbs 20.6, protein 23.2

Crunchy Pork Belly

Preparation Time: 10 minutes

Cooking time: 30 minutes

Servings: 2

Ingredients

9 oz pork belly

1 teaspoon salt

2 tablespoon olive oil

½ teaspoon ground black pepper

Directions:

Sprinkle the pork belly with the salt and ground black pepper.

After this, brush the pork belly with the olive oil.

Preheat the air fryer to 320 F.

Put the pork belly there and cook it for 20 minutes.

After this, increase the temperature to 360 F and cook it for 10 minutes more.

Let the cooked pork belly chill till the room temperature.

Taste it!

Nutrition: calories 710, fat 48.4, fiber 0.1, carbs 0.3, protein 58.9

EASY RECIPES

Roasted Fennel

Preparation Time: 20 minutes

Servings: 4

Ingredients:

1 lb. fennel; cut into small wedges

3 tbsp. olive oil

2 tbsp. sunflower seeds

Juice of ½ lemon

Salt and black pepper to taste.

Directions:

Take a bowl and mix the fennel wedges with all the ingredients except the sunflower seeds, put them in your air fryer's basket and cook at 400°F for 15 minutes

Divide the fennel between plates, sprinkle the sunflower seeds on top and serve as a side dish.

Nutrition: Calories: 152; Fat: 4g; Fiber: 2g; Carbs: 4g; Protein: 7g

Dill Red Cabbage

Preparation Time: 25 minutes

Servings: 4

Ingredients:

30 oz. red cabbage; shredded

4 oz. butter; melted

1 tbsp. red wine vinegar

2 tbsp. dill; chopped.

1 tsp. cinnamon powder

A pinch of salt and black pepper

Directions:

In a pan that fits your air fryer, mix the cabbage with the rest of the ingredients, toss, put the pan in the machine and cook at 390°F for 20 minutes

Divide between plates and serve as a side dish.

Nutrition: Calories: 201; Fat: 17g; Fiber: 2g; Carbs: 5g; Protein: 5g

Rice Salad

Preparation time: 10 minutes

Cooking time: 20 minutes

Servings: 4

Ingredients:

1 cup wild rice

2 cups chicken stock

1 red onion, chopped

1 tablespoon olive oil

Salt and black pepper to the taste

1 tablespoon balsamic vinegar

1 cup cherry tomatoes, halved

½ cup black olives, pitted and halved

1 cup zucchinis, cubed

1 handful basil leaves, chopped

Juice of 1 lime

Zest of 1 lime, grated

Directions:

In your air fryer, combine the rice with the stock, onion and the other ingredients, toss and cook at 370 degrees F for 20 minutes.

Divide into bowls and serve for lunch.

Nutrition: calories 251, fat 8, fiber 4, carbs 14, protein 7

Salmon and Spinach Salad

Preparation time: 10 minutes

Cooking time: 15 minutes

Servings: 4

Ingredients:

1-pound salmon fillets, boneless and cubed

1 red bell pepper, chopped

2 spring onions, chopped

1 cup cherry tomatoes, halved

2 cups baby spinach

Salt and black pepper to the taste

1 tablespoon olive oil

½ cup black olives, pitted and chopped

1/3 cup basil, chopped

Directions:

In your air fryer's pan, combine the salmon with the pepper, onions and the other ingredients, toss and cook at 380 degrees F for 15 minutes. Divide everything into bowls and serve.

Nutrition: calories 251, fat 8, fiber 5, carbs 20, protein 6

Cabbage Stew

Preparation time: 10 minutes

Cooking time: 20 minutes

Servings: 4

Ingredients:

1-pound green cabbage, shredded

1 red onion, sliced

1 tablespoon olive oil

1 cup tomato sauce

1 teaspoon chili powder

1 teaspoon hot paprika

1 teaspoon coriander seeds, crushed

Salt and black pepper to the taste

2 chili peppers, chopped

Directions:

Heat up the air fryer with the oil at 370 degrees F, add the onion and cook for 5 minutes.

Add the cabbage and the other ingredients, toss and cook for 15 minutes.

Divide into bowls and serve for lunch.

Nutrition: calories 251, fat 11, fiber 4, carbs 17, protein 5

Hot Calamari and Spinach Mix

Preparation time: 10 minutes

Cooking time: 20 minutes

Servings: 4

Ingredients:

1 cup calamari rings

1 cup tomatoes, cubed

2 cups baby spinach

2 tablespoons olive oil

1 tablespoon hot sauce

1 tablespoon sweet paprika

1 tablespoon tomato sauce

Salt and black pepper to the taste

1 tablespoon cilantro, chopped

1 tablespoon chives, chopped

Directions:

In your fryer, combine the calamari with the tomatoes, spinach and the other ingredients, toss and cook at 350 degrees F for 20 minutes.

Divide the mix into bowls and serve for lunch.

Nutrition: calories 251, fat 8, fiber 2, carbs 9, protein 15

LOW-COST RECIPES

The Best Fish Tacos Ever

Preparation Time: 25 minutes

Servings: 3

Nutrition: 493 Calories; 19.2g Fat; 48.4g Carbs; 30.8g Protein; 5.8g Sugars

Ingredients

1 tablespoon mayonnaise

1 teaspoon Dijon mustard

1 tablespoon sour cream

1/2 teaspoon fresh garlic, minced

1/4 teaspoon red pepper flakes

Sea salt, to taste

2 bell peppers, seeded and sliced

1 shallot, thinly sliced

1 egg

1 tablespoon water

1 tablespoon taco seasoning mix

1/3 cup tortilla chips, crushed

1/4 cup parmesan cheese, grated

1 halibut fillet, cut into 1-inch strips

6 mini flour taco shells

6 lime wedges, for serving

Directions

Thoroughly combine the mayonnaise, mustard, sour cream, garlic, red pepper flakes, and salt. Add the bell peppers and shallots; toss to coat well. Place in your refrigerator until ready to serve.

Line the Air Fryer basket with a piece of parchment paper.

In a shallow bowl, mix the egg, water, and taco seasoning mix. In a separate shallow bowl, mix the crushed tortilla chips and parmesan.

Dip the fish into the egg mixture, then coat with the parmesan mixture, pressing to adhere.

Bake in the preheated Air Fryer at 380 degrees F for 13 minutes, flipping halfway through the cooking time.

Divide the creamed pepper mixture among the taco shells. Top with the fish and serve with lime wedges. Enjoy!

Savory Cheese and Herb Biscuits

Preparation Time: 30 minutes

Servings: 3

Nutrition: 382 Calories; 22.1g Fat; 35.6g Carbs; 10.3g Protein; 3.1g Sugars

Ingredients

1 cup self-rising flour

1/2 teaspoon baking powder

1/2 teaspoon honey

1/2 stick butter, melted

1/2 cup Colby cheese, grated

1/2 cup buttermilk

1/4 teaspoon kosher salt

1 teaspoon dried parsley

1 teaspoon dried rosemary

Directions

Preheat your Air Fryer to 360 degrees F. Line the cooking basket with a piece of parchment paper.

In a mixing bowl, thoroughly combine the flour, baking powder, honey, and butter. Gradually stir in the remaining ingredients.

Bake in the preheated Air Fryer for 15 minutes.

Work in batches. Serve at room temperature. Bon appétit!

Favorite Spinach Cheese Pie

Preparation Time: 30 minutes

Servings: 4

Nutrition: 521 Calories; 33.9g Fat; 36.1g Carbs; 17.9g Protein; 5.2g Sugars

Ingredients

1 (16-ouncerefrigerated rolled pie crusts

4 eggs, beaten

1/2 cup buttermilk

1/2 teaspoon salt

1/2 teaspoon garlic powder

1/4 teaspoon cayenne pepper

2 cups spinach, torn into pieces

1 cup Swiss cheese, shredded

2 tablespoons scallions, chopped

Directions

Unroll the pie crust and press it into a cake pan, crimping the top edges if desired.

In a mixing dish, whisk together the eggs, buttermilk, salt, garlic, powder, and cayenne pepper.

Add the spinach, 1/2 of Swiss cheese, and scallions into the pie crust; pour the egg mixture over the top. Sprinkle the remaining 1/2 cup of Swiss cheese on top of the egg mixture.

Bake in the preheated Air Fryer at 350 degrees F for 10 minutes. Rotate the cake pan and bake an additional 10 minutes.

Transfer to a wire rack to cool for 5 to 10 minutes. Serve warm.

Greek-Style Pizza with Spinach and Feta

Preparation Time: 20 minutes

Servings: 2

Nutrition: 502 Calories; 29.5g Fat; 53.6g Carbs; 14.8g Protein; 17.3g Sugars

Ingredients

2 ounces frozen chopped spinach

Coarse sea salt, to taste

2 personal pizza crusts

1 tablespoon olive oil

1/4 cup tomato sauce

2 tablespoons fresh basil, roughly chopped

1/2 teaspoon dried oregano

1/2 feta cheese, crumbled

Directions

Add the frozen spinach to the saucepan and cook until all the liquid has evaporated, about 6 minutes. Season with sea salt to taste.

Preheat the Air Fryer to 395 degrees F.

Unroll the pizza dough on the Air Fryer baking tray; brush with olive oil.

Spread the tomato sauce over the pizza crust. Add the sautéed spinach, basil, and oregano. Sprinkle the feta cheese, covering the pizza crust to the edges.

Cook for 10 minutes, rotating your pizza halfway through the cooking time. Repeat with another pizza and serve warm.

CONCLUSION

Thank you for reading all this book!

Cleaning the air fryer is easy and it does not require you to do a lot of complicated tasks. The first thing that you need to do is to unplug the air fryer before cleaning to prevent electrocution. The basket is dishwasher-friendly, so you can take it out from the fryer's chamber and clean them in the sink or in the dishwasher

You have already taken a step towards your improvement.

Best wishes!